Sifting Sound into Shape

Meditations in prose and poetry
by Dónall Dempsey

Sifting Sound into Shape

Dónall Dempsey

1st edition

ISBN: 978-1-907435-10-2

www.dempseyandwindle.co.uk

Contents

About the Writing

The Poems

A kind of Intro...I guess?

Despite the little accent on the ó telling them just where to go -
people always mispronounce my name... aghhhhhhhh the pain! Ain't
it plain!

My name in Gaelic translates as:
'World Mighty! ' or 'Spear Power! '

...so, I'm sticking to it: so there! (I won't get a name like it again) .

.My second name Dempsey (O' Diomsaigh) translates as:
'The Proud One! '

So, call me by my name!

'World Mighty Spear Power The Proud One! '

'Ain't it the truth...ain't it the truth! ' as the Cowardly Lion would
say. Bit difficult to live up to at times! But actually the truth is
this...an Irish sense of humour! Yes...nothing more...nothing less.
Impressed?
No... neither was I!

I was a mere slip of a boy when I was born...weighing in at an
enormous...two pounds! My belly weighs that now all by itself! So
what do you call the littlest baby you've ever seen...why...'World
Mighty! ' of course. Of course...there's that Irish sense of humour
and wonder.

When I was born they didn't have any incubators and so they used
to have to wrap me up in cotton wool to keep me warm. I used to
hate the stuff and would shuffle out of it at every opportunity!
That's how I learnt how to wiggle so well....even now if you were to
wrap my nakedness in cotton wool...well... I'd outta there in a flash.
A skill I will have until I shuffle off this mortal coil. I'm just a
natural talent.

'Man... it's the weird white stuff again...just what do they think they're playing at...sh** man, I mean...don't do that! "

I guess I'm just a natural nudist...when I came to my birth...I just came as I was.

Weighing no more than a bag of sugar I would disappear in my Dad's mighty hand with just two little legs no bigger than thumbs sticking out.

A nurse with a sleight of hand did this disappearing trick and chuckled: 'He's so small Mrs. Dempsey...I'm gonna drown him in that pot of geraniums! ' To her horror my mother pleaded for my life ('Oh no sister...don't! ') and proceeded to haemorrhage massively. To her horror the poor nurse didn't know what to do and almost fainted with me in hand but as you see I survived all these attempts on my life.

Above our bed in the hospital ward was a painting of the Sacred Heart (you Catholics know the one.. the one with Jesus tearing open his clothes like Superman to reveal his thorn encrusted burning heart and following you everywhere with those never leaving you eyes) and this was the first thing I seen after I woke up from being borned.

I could only assume (aw come on... I was only a couple of hours old...how was I to know) that this was my Dad... so I thought I was the son of Christ! Christ...what a mistake!

Anti-Christ more like as my mother would say.

I had arrived ready to party and I had come prepared. I had heard the sound that that Elvis guy(was he the son of Christ if not me?) had made and I nearly slithered off the labour ward table I came out so fast...I almost hit the ground running! I was a well held baseball at an all important moment in an all important game. Well held...sister! I had long black sideburns(see I had done my research) and I was all shock up... uh huh.. uh huh...oh yeah!

But when I got there it was...Doris Day! I checked to see if I had got the right mother but yup...she was mine all right! I was the first boy after three girls and my mother desperately wanted me(well...not me particularly...I guess any boy would do but she was stuck with me) .

She pleaded with Doc Carroll to: '.. make it a boy...please...will it be a boy doctor! '

And he said: 'I don't f*******know...Eta... whatever will f******be will f******be! '

As it happened this was the song playing on the labour ward radio as I made my escape from my mother where I had holed up inside for all of seven months. So I came to be... accompanied by the best selling 45 of the moment. And so Doris was my first love! Being born was like taking a sentimental journey and she was my secret love. I was a breech birth...so as I put first one and then two cautious toes out into the world to test the water...what quickly followed after...confirmed my manhood.

My mother said: 'I don't care what pain I now undergo as long as I know...it's a boy! ' And then she said: 'aghhhhhhh....agHHHHHH! ! '

She's been a good mother to me and I was glad to have her present at my birth...I don't know what I would have done without her! I still ring her up on my birthday and thank her for having me...after all she did all the hard worked and I simply went with the flow. O happy day: yeah...right!

Our Irish names mean a lot to us and they always mean something more than just the thing you use to call us in for our dinner or to say 'Stop pulling that cat's tail! ' or 'If you fall off that wall and hurt yourself...I'll kill ya! ' or 'Dónall...Dónall...what are you doing...well...stop it...whatever it is...that you're doing...right now...or else...right...that's it...don't say I didn't tell you...you're in for it now! '

My sister's name is Bláthin Aisling and she was only a pound and a couple of ounces but they had incubators by the time she decided to born herself. Bláth means flower in Irish and Bláthin means little flower. Aisling means dream or vision. So her name means: 'Dream of a little flower' 'Little flower dream.' I love her name. I love her.

When she was born she was dead.

Nobody out of all the many doctors gathered around the bed could find the tiny heartbeat 'though they hunted for it with stethoscopes and all kinds of complicated machinery. They assumed the baby was dead inside her and told her so. She turned and cried to the pillow as they all stood around in their white coats not knowing what to do with this woman's grief. An Indian doctor who had nothing whatsoever to do with the proceedings just happened to be passing and asked if he may try. They smirked at his foolishness. He took an immaculate white handkerchief out of his top pocket and like a magician spread it upon my mother's belly. He warmed his hands so that the 'dear lady, will not feel cold.' He placed his ear to the handkerchief and listened intently for a sound...the littlest of sound. He smiled gently and like a magic trick whipped away the handkerchief with the baby's heartbeat safe within it. He had conjured her up...snatched her from her death before her birth. She was only the littlest of sounds.

When she was born... she was dead.

They put her aside in the place where you put dead babies aside. They told my mother that she would have to name the child. My mother looked out of her tears out of the window out into the morning. It was a dawn being born and outside on the lawn was a little flower bravely battling the winds of this new day and trying hard to hold on to its fragile petals. My mother called her dead daughter...little flower. Bláthin. And she had such a short dream of being alive that she called her...dream. Aisling. Bláthin Ashling. A vision...a dream.

Her dead daughter was to be called Bláthin Aisling. No one would ever know or love her except her...forever and ever. Right now forever had died in this useless dawn...this broken morning...that had somehow found them amongst all the threads of entangled time.

Just then...nothing to do with anything...he just happened to be passing...yet again. The Indian doctor refused to believe that his magic could have failed and refused to accept the death of this little flower. He went to where they had bought her...took her into his hands...his breath upon her... willed her to live. He slapped her hard on the bottom and a weak cry greeted his beautifully manicured hands. He forced life upon her and she accepted as best as her tiny littleness could. She was brown as a berry as if she had taken some of his colour into her skin. She grew up to be my little sister...best footballer on the boy's team when girls didn't ever play on the boy's team but they couldn't do without her.. she was their top scorer. And she was a champion javelin thrower.

She is a fairy story all of her own. An Indian doctor is a prince who can breath life into death. Now continents and years apart he has probably gone on to meet his death and she is still living the life he bestowed upon her.

Whenever I hear the sound of my sister's name the whole story of her birth flashes before me and I see a man's life giving hands.

When she was born...she was dead...but now she lives her life with little blonde kids that look so much like her. The little baby now has her little babies.

And so, a name, as you can see... is not just there to call you in for your tea but to call you into being...call you into life.. .

In ancient Celtic times along with the name you would be known as...your mother with her first breast milk would whisper your secret name into your innocent ear...a name known only to her and to you in your present state of unknowing...knowing everything and nothing. And only when you had grown to your death and forgotten all that the child had known...and had ceased to be the God you were when you were born...would a God or whatever means the Good come and call you by your secret name...known only to you and your mother and no...other.

'Love...love! ' he would call you and your death would answer: 'Here I am! '

For the secret name of all humans despite whatever sound or syllables it is spelt or spilt in...is...love... only love.

It is love that makes us. . .human.

....

About the Writing

Writing SAFE IN THE ARMS OF JESUS

Although these poems exist alone they also form a sequence so I have threaded them together to form this necklace of poems.

They are in memory of a lovely woman I used to look after who not only didn't know her own name but didn't know who she was or where she was. You had to keep eye contact with her at all times otherwise she would forget who you were and start to scream:

'Agghhh...there's a man...there's a man! ' '

Who...where? ' I'd say and she'd say: 'You...you! '

I'd say: 'No, I'm Donall and you're Breda...remember? '

And she'd say: 'You are...? '

'I'm Donall...! ' she'd say and I'd say: 'No, you're...! '

A name and who you were...only a yellow sticky label that fell off and got put back on the wrong object. Words not meaning anything anymore...only sounds.

And this losing of me and of her self went on all through the day...we would have to be (collectively or individually) found again and again throughout our time together...looking for an identify like looking for a lost shoe.

Although she had no memory she would continually and forever return to one moment in the past (July 1939) and remember in exact detail all that happened in that one glorious time of being in love and the world stretching out in front of her with no end in sight. The war was just a storm cloud moving in on a sunny day. She remembers being on her belly and the grass tickling and annoying her through her summer frock. She remembers that it started to rain...little drop by little drop building up into big fat droplets...and that one of the drops fell on the page she was reading(P.49) and enclosed the word 'crying' in a little prism. The word magnified itself...she never was able to tell me what she was reading only that it was poetry:

'Poetry, dear...I only read poetry, dear! '

Her 'chap' came up quietly behind her and kissed her...she put her arms around his neck and he pulled her up like that...locked in the kiss and the embrace. They walked hand in hand among the dead trying to make out the past lives that had been lived long ago. Someone called their names and they turned and became...that photo. She still had it over her mantlepiece. It was her one and only possession... she didn't even own her own nightgown or her clothes...they were the hospital's. All he had was this photo and that memory. When she died the photo was thrown out into the bin. She died amongst a storm that raged against the living one night and she escaped peacefully into sleep and death with hardly a murmur.

She was very guilty of calling her lover Jesus('Jesus Jones') and she felt maybe that his death was God's punishment on her. She read a tombstone that said someone so long ago had fallen asleep in the arms of Jesus'...a poetic way of announcing Death. She had said to him: 'I want to fall asleep in your arms...you're my Jesus! ' The nickname and the private game stuck and he remained ever so for ever...Jesus Jones.

I try to bring them back and show their great love and that beautiful day that so remained in her mind until she too was gathered up and fell asleep in the arms of the only man she would ever love or know...
Jesus Jones.

Their love is a beautiful jewel and shines always in my mind.

Writing KUTENI, MTA' KWETU?

This poem was brought into being one night hearing my friend
Kevin recite his DESPERATE BOY poem. It got to the lines:

He owns a lost poem...

A 100 butterflies

In the shape of a miracle

Hover a foot above his bed

(by Kevin Reinhardt)

And the tears just came and I realised that I too had a lost poem
(that just had to be written if it were the last thing I'd do) and it
appeared to me like: "a 100 butterflies in the shape of a miracle."
As I sat there being caressed by his voice...my lost poem...began to
hover a foot above my head...as if I were a cartoon of a man about
to write a poem and the words were being encapsulated in a speech
bubble that floated off in the applause that greeted my friend's
poem. As I travelled home that night to Barking on the last tube...it
was eerily empty and the carriages seemed to be rocked around like
a broken toy in a child's hand. A wind blew newspapers like leaves
scattered around the carriage. All the papers had been torn into
pieces as if they had been savaged by a werewolf who couldn't read
and so had angrily ripped them to shreds. I usually never(ever)
travel anywhere without a book in a bag but this night...I was
bookless! Desperate to read anything... anything... I picked up the
nearest shred and read:

KUTENI, MTA' KWETU?

ZULU(XHOSA DIALECT)

("WHAT'S THE MATTER...OUR CHILD? ")

The title intrigued me and I searched the entire carriage for the
remnants of the article it had come from but alas...it was not to be

found. Maybe the illiterate werewolf had taken this one scrap to study it and see if he could learn to read.

A full moon laughed in a carriage window.

The construction of the question was the same as it would be in Ireland, Liverpool or Yorkshire...with all the familiarity and tenderness falling on the phrase "...our child! "

A full moon laughed and the night asked once again:

"KUTENI, MTA' KWETU? "

"WHAT'S THE MATTER...OUR CHILD? "

Once again tears came and I felt the great beyond was asking me why I cried...of what I cried...of whom I cried for. The answer was a simple and inescapable howl...my soul torn into shreds and floating with the pieces of paper that danced around the empty seats. I was so alone and incapable of any speech...I could only speak in tears.

....

Writing WE ARE LEGEND...WE ARE MYTH

My Uncle Seanie was straight out of OF MICE AND MEN...big and strong but simple and beautiful as a child. He'd take the big dray horse out of the huge cart and pull us along himself. Dolly was glad of the rest and if the human wanted to do her job then...let him. She laughed and chomped grass. Standing upright (me a little seven year old boy) in the palm of his hand I would travel the world of field after field in this magical manner totally transported by his strength and delight. It was like being a bird but standing still at the same time...the world transformed by this seeing. And if he should stumble and fall and I fell...why he'd catch me and transfer me laughing to his shoulders without breaking his stride. His name was Seanie but he should have been called "Love." Just "Love." He cracked open the world and let all its treasures pour forth and I was rich indeed. He was my genie! And anything was possible.

"Seanie! "

This poem was written not with words but with tears. I had no pen or paper so I wrote it in my head as we hurtled into the night...the moon trying desperately to keep up with us. I cried it out to the carriage of no-one and to the only person I wanted to hear it:

"Seanie! "

When I finally came to read the poem in public it almost broke my heart and I had to leave the room immediately.

I cried all the way home yet again. The pain of this has always haunted me and the poem is a sad attempt to acknowledge the hurt I done to him.

I know he would only have taken me in his arms...wrapping me up in those big strong arms and smothered me in love and a bear-sized hug.

Every night I still travel with him through fields held in the palm of his hand above his head seeing the world unfurl in this way or riding his shoulders as if by some magic of the Greek gods we had been transformed into that mythical creature...the centaur...half man/half horse/half boy/half man....the legendary being known only as "Dónall! Seanie! " or "Seanie! Dónall! " galloping out of sight of the spite and hurt in my Auntie's voice.

As you see it has also become a short story that I wrote for my brother Brian because he remembered Seanie and loved him as much as I...different memories... different times... but still that great big love of a great big man.

Ballea was the name of the magical farm we would only see in summer on holiday and indeed the farm danced and was covered in honeysuckle and roses. It was the special place. In any Dempsey mind its name is just sheer magic... capable of summoning up the ghosts and spirits of what is past and what has come to past although it now lies in ruins.

Manchester Untied (especially the 1968 team) are poetry in motion. Names like George Best (yes he was the best), Denis Law (almost a myth) and Bobby Charlton (spellbinding) were magical charms... even to only utter their names! This was the team that won the European Cup in honour of the team that died in the 1956 Munich air disaster. That final was the resolve of their deaths and hugely emotional. We cried that we won and we cried for the dead.

Bill Shankly said "Football is not a matter of life and death...it's more important than that! "

Wall football (a consolation to the solitary child) is played in your head as much as outdoor as the ball rebounds and rebounds and you become all your heroes at once. It would be played non-stop for hours on end into the late evenings until your mother unable to stand the pounding anymore sent you to bed. It was a combination of imagination and physicality and you become totally immersed and lost in it. It was this private world that Seanie bungled into.

Writing PARALLEL LINES DON'T MEET

About five years ago working with challenging kids I got my arm broken and had only recovered from that when I received a head injury which took out the other arm and paralysed the left hand side of my face. The next five years were a long day's journey into night and sheer agony and I became a ghost haunting my own life. I had to learn how to speak properly again (still with an Irish accent) and it took a year for me to be able to close my eye again and another 6 months before I could blink and wink at you.

This is my whistling past the graveyard poem with me hoping that the light at the end of the tunnel was the the light at the end of the tunnel and not another oncoming train.

I had forgotten what happy was.

Before the pain and paralysis rushed me I took a step back and like an American football player I threw my happiness up into the air and ran forward into my future to try and meet it. The ball seemed like it would never come down but...my happiness finally came to ground in the form of this lovely lady. It was touchdown and my *ecstatic* heart went wild.

I know now what happy is.

A woman called ... Janice.

YOUR LITTLEST SMILE

Death, rather diffident (rather shy)

comes to me & says: "It is time to die!"

"Ok..." I say ". . .when?"

"Now. . .like, this moment…this…second!"

I struggle with my heart attack

as Death

(feeling bad about it)

repossess my artefacts.

Outside a van pulls up with neat Gothic script

DEATH – REMOVALS

it spells out in big bold letters.

I like it.

Death's got style(and a nice smile)

and is a kind of groovy guy.

Or is he. . . a lady...boy...it's hard to tell.

This heart attack hurts like hell.

"Ok boys – take it all away!"

Death's little helpers(all big bruisers all over 6' 2")

former nightclub bouncers.

They take away the blue sky

under which I had first kissed you.

They take away the little day to day things I always loved

. . .the shape of your mouth

your continuously falling hair brushed impatiently away

from your eyes. . .your eyes

The smell of your perfume in an empty room

the littlest of your smiles I had saved for a rainy day.

Meanwhile like a living Houdini . . .I had done it.

Somehow wrestled out of

the heart attack's straitjacket.

"Damn!" Death

spat in a peevish manner.

"How in God's name did you do that?"

Death sighed: "Ok kid, ya got me. . .this time!"

"Right boys...put it all back. . . put everything back!"

Les Boys, scowled at me

as if to say: "I'll remember you . . .sunny Jim!"

"You. . !" Death

snarled from the side of his mouth

annoyed now(no more Mr. Nice guy)

"You. . !" "I'll see you. . .again!"

A tear...trickled down my cheek (unable to speak)

all I could do was glance down

your littlest smile

clasped tightly in my hand.

AS GAEILGE - IN IRISH

Dún do shúile *(Close your eyes)*

Codail go lá...mo ghrá séimh. *(Sleep until day...my gentle love)*.

Codail go sámh go sámh. *(Sleep peacefully...peacefully)*.

Éirdeoidh an ghealach seo... ...is rachaidh an ghrian seo faoi *(This moon will rise... ...this sun will set)*

aire 'gus grá i gconaí *(care and love always)*

gach oíche 's gach lá gach lá 's gach oíche.

(every night every day every day every night)

Mo phlúirín! Mo stóirín! Mo mhuirnín!

(My little flower! My little treasure! My little darling!)

Ach anois... *(But now...)*

codail go sámh go séimh *(sleep peacefully...gently)*

go fáinne an lae *(until the break of day)*

le mise ar do taobh *(with me by your side)*.

Losing our baby late into the night

holding this...little thing...that only attempted to be human

unable to let go

I clasped the foetus tightly in my hand

& buried it in the dawn of our local park

under a recently planted red rose bush.

In my grief flower & baby

became one

and night after night I climbed

over high railings & even higher stars

to talk to her in the dark .... in Irish.

Or sing: My Love is like a Red Red Rose.

Or cry...or...cry.

Almost got arrested one night by an Irish cop

drawn to the sound of Irish emerging from darkness.

Guess he let me go because it wouldn't look good

on a charge sheet:

"The defendant was talking & crying to...a flower."

- in Irish.

Eist...eist *(listen...listen)*

duinne eagin ag caoineadh *(someone is crying)*

in a dorchasan *(in his darkness).*

Fill...fill...a run o!

Fill a run o is na imigh uaim.

Fill orm a chuisle a stor

agus chifeadh tu an gloire... ma fhillean tu!

I FEEL PRETTY... OH SO... PRETTY!

I a......wake
covered in glorious glitter smelling strongly of PVA glue

sticking to my cheek very hung over
& covered in blueorangeyellowred feathers

a bubble recently blown perched upon my nose
I...still....half coma...tose

tiny bubbles travel amongst my curls
as through a bigger bubble brightly
nestling neatly over my right eye

I observe my tiny daughter purse her lips & kiss
more bubbles into being.

"Till...y! "

I force my lips(still frozen in sleep) to some how speak:
"What...you...do? "

(even my syntax and sentence structuring is shot)

She smiles sweetly: "I'm...pretty-ing you!"

COME DANCING

I take the skeleton's hand & man ... do we dance?

I clasp his bony hand in mine
give him a high five and dude...we jive!

No one can touch us now (we're in a world of our own) .

We shake, rattle 'n' roll...yeah! Shake, rattle 'n' roll (then we)
Git into dat kitchen 'n' rattle 'em pots 'n' pans Den den den...den!

The skeleton flashes me a toothy grin.
"Man ... you the one ... you the one ... what a groove ... we're in! "

The transistorised air is alive as song after song drives me on.

The skeleton don't break sweat!
Me...my scalp prickles...sweat trickles down my spine.

Sunlight spills in the window & the dust motes go wild.

The skeleton places a bony hand on my clavicle
& I place my hand on his sacroiliac.

We waltz eye socket to eye socket & patella to patella.

Gene Kelly sings:

What a great day it's been... what a rare mood I'm in
why it's... almost like being in love!

He's a fine medical specimen.

He dangles from a thread in his head
& the slightest breeze moves him...gets him going.

I call him Mr. Bo Jangles.
He lives in my Dad's army sport stores.

From the inner sanctum of his room
my Dad's army voice booms:

"Donall...leave that bloody skeleton alone! "
And goes back to counting his balls.

The ledger grows & grows.
(He mutters & mumbles to himself).

"Balls...soccer...50? ...50!. . .Balls... rugby...50? ...50! "
"Balls...medicine...50? ...50! "
he intones as if chanting a mantra.

I shuffle out...trying to be cool (in this heat?)
"Yo, see ya later Bo! "

Years later I see him

in a tiny newspaper article.

Apparently the Army
realise they've got a real life skeleton on their hands

& decide to do the decent thing
(remembering the man he'd been)

& bury him
with full military honours

flag draped coffin & shots fired into the air
scaring the crows away.

I wish I could have...been there.

Say my goodbyes.

I smile & whisper a little prayer:

"Yo, see ya later...Bo! "

THE GHOST CLUB

It's THE GHOST CLUB

you hardly know when you're dead
it's just a different kind of alive

I hang around my old shed
touch & not touch my rusting tools

some of the other ghosts hang out at the bandstand
but only when it rains

we call ourselves THE GHOST CLUB
chat 'bout this 'n' that…that 'n' this

you know the little things that make a life
we keep in touch with the living

shadowing them…pretending to be their shadow
hidden in a sudden slant of sun on an evening

we shout and shout but our words are invisible

it's like living in a parallel dimension

living inside a snow dome

when it's turned up side down the fake snow falling
mimicking the real snow falling gently now outside

I'd love to cry but I've forgotten how
and I don't know if it's allowed

it's a life of sorts somehow. . .I get by(I miss my boy)

bye…bye. . .bye

TARAB
(FOR ONELIA)

The words come to me demanding to be written
& are bitterly disappointedto find that I am

me
not
you.

Somehow, they had managed to turn up in the wrong head
mistaking me for you because I was thinking so much of you.

Too late now they come to realize their mistake.
Reluctantly they agree to stay & be this poem.

I can see they are not impressed.

Missing Bulgaria & ending up in England in an Irish head
is bad but badder still geting the sex wrong & being this guy!

A word breaks down begins to cry.

'She's got what the Arabs call tarab! '
one word is heard to remark.

"Yes...yes it's that intoxication of the senses beyond all reason! '
another word elucidates....almost hallucinates.

'Hey shit for brains! '
a bunch of words cruelly calls

'Onelia would have written us better than this! '

Some words try to hide

in the space between the lines.

Some words hide in the surrounding empty space
refusing to come out or even talk about ... 'it! '

Some words live lives of quiet desperation
silently erasing themselves.

Some words hijack this page & turning it into a paper airplane
demand to be taken to Sofia.

They are already incensed to have missed your birthday.

So, if by your dreaming head a paper airplane appears
full of frustrated distraught words

take them - they are yours.

You the better poet than I could ever be.

You...the great you...me...merely me.

*DUSO

This star
was born with you

enclosed
within your breast

(it is your namesake)

to follow you
through life

and die only with
your own death.

Burn brightly

with the love
you are

made of.

Burn brightly

make love
the only thing

worth
living for.

*Duso....meaning "Love"...but literally "Soul" in Serbian.

In Serbian mythology we are all born with a star that goes with us
through life and leaves us with our Death.

TEAR BY TEAR
(for Onelia)

At night I visit the village
in which I was born.

I float above rooftops
dive into the house next door

to my own
little home

swim down streets with all the swagger
of a fish amongst coral reefs.

It lies to the northwest
but is submerged

beneath the waters
behind a dam.

Each night I visit it
leaving my body behind

drifting in dreams
diving beneath the waters

of the Past
(swimming where) I used to walk

trying to remake it

memory by memory

tear by tear.

KUTENI MTA', KWETU?

('What's The Matter, Our Child? ')

I am the entire 1968 Manchester United team!

The ball ricochets against the wall & I leap to meet
the perfect cross(to head home) the perfect goal.

But...

Uncle Seanie simple as a child
(since the day his Dad died) has me foiled.

He plucks the ball from its near perfect trajectory & I
head nothing at all & fall.

His awkward miskick stupidly sticks
in the thickest hedge of thorns that can be found.

A loud hiss tells of the ball's imminent demise.

Enraged I scold him like a childlike a scalded pup
& see the hurt stain his eyes.

He is heartily sorry for having offended me
& oh my God he turns & like Frankenstein's monster

strides into the...plunges into the thick of the thorns.

Christ like he emerges like a resurrection
his face torn & cut...blood...tears trickling down his face.

"Here's your ball boy. . .I'm sorry! "

The ball transformed into nothing but what
resembles a human heart

that he holds in his hands and asks for forgiveness.

The child looks at the child in his eyes
& childishly scorns him.

My Uncle's eyes hold the hurt
useless as a broken toy.

He walks after me begging my forgiveness
that will... not come.

And now, forever I walk after him
begging for forgiveness

that can never come.

THE FLAG OF ITSELF

the bell
empties itself
creates silence

the flower
unfurls the flag
of itself

the bird sings
to the rain
darkness whispers to the sky

the wind
chases the grass
all over itself

her skirt
brushes raindrops from the grass
the ascent of a lark

RIVER RUN PAST ADAM & EVE'S

Fascinated with the bright coloured pages
I would walk through the world of the atlas

tearing the earth apart.

I only ever took rivers
tore them out with my bare hands

from source to estuary
in a ecstasy of creativity

their long writhing blue lines with towns and lands clinging to it
on either side tributaries dangling like blue veins .

All the great rivers flowed upon
our waxy shiny living room table

my face like a great god's reflected in it

as if this was a river's waiting room in Heaven
where rivers hung around and wriggled

. . .until God decided where to put 'em.

The Nile lay curled up at the edges
entwined around a pot of pink geraniums.

The Mississippi tore in two..by mistake!

The Amazon falling on the ground
lost among toys and shoes various rubbish & bric-a-brac.

Now, I had control
over all the great rivers in the world

they lay there panting reflected on the table
coiled like wild tamed snakes!

The empty spaces of where they had been in the atlas
(a parallel universe)where nothing flowed

only the torn out empty spaces
in the shape of rivers...no longer there!

I would stick them in on the white pages of my scrapbook
which I had entitled in my best/worst joined up handwriting

RIVERS OF THE WORLD I HAVE KNOWN.

When a windy night unlocked the window
(and blew the rivers of the world into turmoil)

the Nile clinging timidly to a curtain

the Mississippi making a run for it

out of the open window vanishing into the night!

And then my mother's voice
exclaiming: "Look...at all the mess you've made! "

And I (the great riverer of the world) was sent to bed.

The rivers crawling up the stairs
a little later after the house had fallen asleep

sneaking into my dreams
filling up my head.

AGAINST THE BRIGHTNESS OF TIME

She doesn't know she has a year left
... to live.

She is a photograph shielding her eyes
against the brightness of Time.

She is looking into the Future
to see if she can see me.

She has not been introduced to her Death (as yet)
but it...knows her.

She will never see this photograph that holds her so
tenderly as if it loved her.

It comes from an undeveloped roll
left over in a dusty back drawer

that only came to light years later.

An unknown roll that gave birth to these photos that now stand
in the photo frames of those who had loved her.

She looks back at me now in disbelief
that she has become just this photo

a little scrap of memory caught on the barbwire of Time
struggling in my mind to break free

her voice(stealing through Time)

still asking the question: 'Do you love me...? '

I telling the photograph:
'I do! '

COMMUNION

new dress
she stands on kitchen table
finishing touches to hem

"Stand still...stand still!"
she's got
pins and needles

Mum hums
her smile
full of pins

SIFTING SOUND INTO SHAPE

"S"
he scrawled silently
(tongue in cheek).

"ILE"
the pencil pondered ponderously
(an awesome feat) .

"NT"
his head empty
(...empty...)

"LY"
"You've got to try! "
(He could only cry)

a prism of tears
enclosing the word
(a microbe microscopically magnified)
by his despair.

The black markings that he made
would not talk back to him.

He saw only the silent white
that glowed around each lonely letter

felt only the emptiness that writing cut out
of the page's snowdrift.

He could not claim to know how
letters chiseled meaning into words

until once
(suddenly it seemed)
upon a time

sifting shape into sense

there fell through the mesh of letters
nuggets of words golden with meaning.

"Gold! "
stuttered his stunted pencil.

"Gold! "
his startled hand mimed.

"Gold! "
screamed his mind.

"Gold! "

"Gold! "

"Gold! "

SHARING WING BIRDS

A moon
the colour of sorrow.

Rain falling
like regret.

The memory
of your beauty

awakened by
the music

tiptoes on moonlit feet
slowly silently

across the lawn.

A cat
(immune to human emotion)
yawns

silhouetted against
an Autumn moon.

He listens
to our human words

more out of boredom
than anything else

as if we were characters
in a play

enacting words that will be
forever spoken:

'Let us be sharing wing birds

...the thing of legend...

with only one eye
only one wing

only by sharing wings
can we fly! '

Chiseled into
a night gone by

the words remain
engraved upon the air.

The cat wonders
how do humans do that

...& why?

He pads quietly
through the words

the memory of us
bristling his fur.

MOTHERING INSTINCT

Tears...tears well but don't fall.

Bottom lip. . .trembles.
Top lip. . . quivers

& just before she can begin
to howl......I howl!

I open my mouth & - bawl!

Stunned she stares at my open mouth
with nothing but sobs coming out.

'I'm...cryin'...'cos...you were.....gonna...cry! '

I manage to blurt out
(trying not to laugh behind my crocodile tears).

She climbs up on my lap
(a sturdy little foot on each patella)

wipes my fake tears away with her hair.

'Ah...Dónall Dónall...not cry! '
'Big boy not cry! Sillly...Dónall cry! '

'Shhhhhhhh! 'she shushes me
kissing a me(guilty)

of unleashing my four year old's
mothering instinct.

SAFE IN THE ARMS OF JESUS – SEQUENCE

Jesus fondles her left breast.

'Stop it! Stop it! ' she scolds.
'You're making me ... wet! '

They walk among the broken tombstones
deciphering the moss-eaten inscriptions.

Her summer dress clings to her
as she clings to him.

Someone calls their names
and they turn and-

- their photograph is taken.

Ivy clings to the wall and climbs.
It is July - 1939.

'I called him Jesus(was that bad of me?)
because he was my Saviour.'

'Jesus Jones...'

'I would have died for him but - he died on me.'

'The War got him...he never came home...'

The home help smiles warily
at the little old lady

unable to comprehend the love of then...
because she only sees

...the time of now.

NOW DEATH SEEMS VERY FAR AWAY

It is July - 1939.

Her hair tumbles across her smile.
He shades his eyes against sunlight as if saluting.

Knowing they are going to have their photograph taken:
they stiffen into the postures & positions

that will hold them still forever

as if a facing a firing squad they stand and stare
at a Future they will never share.

Shot through the heart with time.
(Shot through the heart with time).

Never again will it be July - 1939.

THE OLD LADY DREAMS

She ran and ran and
(chased by the Hounds of Death)
until they ran her to earth:

'Ah, my grave! ' she said.

And pulling back the earth lay down and went asleep
in the arms of - Jesus!

Then she - woke up.

She always woke up just as......she snuggled into him.

Sad to be - alive again:
she spat: 'Aw, shit...!

WEATHER FORECAST

A shadow falls upon an open book
a breeze turns the pages

a raindrop falls on the seventh line of page 49
(enclosing the word 'crying') .

It is July - 1939.

We fall in love on a sunny day turned cloudy
turned windy turned rainy

as if all these things had been
preordained

and all we had to do was
me to be me you to be you

as if we had
entered another dimension

where we didn't have to ask
why, or how or whatever

and love(Love)
was the only weather!

SILENCE SHYLY

Midnight drunk throws a brick
through cake shop window

... steals a display wedding cake
almost twice. . .as big as himself.

The alarm is hysterical.
Broken glass looks bloody in neon.

Staggers down the street clutching it to his breast
whilst attempting to eat it.

He shouts:
"This tastes like shite!"

And he's right it only being a work of art
not a real cake one can almost taste.

Three cop cars scream to the rescue.

Tell him to:
"Put the cake down...put the cake down!"

"I'm getting married in the moaning!"

He sings as he is stuffed
into the back of a patrol car.

Silence shyly
tiptoes...back

saying nothing of what has just happened
'cept: "Shhhhh....shhhh....shhhhh!"

A MEMORY OF MOON & WATER

I can still touch
with the fingertip of memory

your Venetian laughter

losing itself in the mist
of Myth & History

here where Past & Present
are one

& my lips kiss your lips
& your heart under my hand

trembles like a tiny frightened bird
that would fly away into a Future

that neither of us know as yet

only the beauty of the moment
the simple thrill

of your hand held in mine
held still in a forever of time

the trace of your Venetian laughter
a memory of moon & water.

PARALLEL LINES DO NOT MEET

Happiness...is not...a mathematical formula
that one can apply to supply an answer.

Rather...it is the sum of who you are
multiplied by who you are willing to be.

Happiness...like Mathematics
is something I was never ever any good at

& always made me weep

with equal parts

Desperation
Exasperation
&
Frustration.

Or DEF for short.

For example:

If it took a man a lifetime
to dig himself into a hole

how long would it take
for half the man he used to be
to dig himself out again?

Questions – such as this
only caused me grief.

In Mathematics (like Latin)
which I could also never know

I would cheat & repeat
words full of sound & no sense.

E.g.

The cares of the hippopotamus
are equal to some of the cares
that the other two hippopotami confide.

Happiness...like Mathematics
was all Greek to me.

I don't know...that's all I know.

But I do know that...
Happiness happens

every now...& then...

the only trick
is to be aware that it's there & that...

Parallel Lines do meet ... at Infinity

Q.E.D.

RECIPE

Take one bed.

Place before an open window
letting it shimmer in summer.

Gently cover in crisp cool linen.
Fluff two white plump pillows.

Now add a little lilac and a light top sheet.

Simmer from high noon to full moon.

Stir in the longing(just a pinch of lust)
not too much...not too much...that's enough!

Now, only now, add the lovers.
Let them stew in their own juices.
Then turn up the heat & serve hot.

Mmmm...a dish fit for the Gods!

SAD VALENTINES FOR BREAKFAST

Oh my how red cock struts (thinks he's a sultan)
striding in and out among his harem-scarum hens

talking to themselves like some lost senile sentimental souls
foolish fowl

they lay eggs for gentlemen and kids on long hot summer holidays

they hide their eggs like broken hearts
like old love letter secrets

safe in unseen places.

But see Auntie Nellie willy-nilly as a fox
stalk the chickens and expose them

cruel as the NEWS OF THE WORLD.

See her raid the haystacks
(back seat of the old car) rain rusting machinery

her apron pregnant and precious with
the warm and brown gift of eggs.

Red Cock crows
loud against the morning marigolds

while children's voices babble sleepily
into wide-awakefulness

love letter secrets staining their lips
sad valentines for breakfast.

A MIDSUMMER'S NIGHT TRAIN RIDE

It could only be...Puck
he & I both...gotten older
our magics deserting us

he smells of wee & wealth
keeps repeating himself
him self. . .him. . .self

he sits inside
his skin & name
as if they don't fit him

"I'm a patient man...patient man!"
he repeats &
repeats impatiently

"Been a member of the Labour Party
from the year zero & I'll die
a member of the year zero!"

"I'm in love
with her Majesty the Queen
always have been...always have been

"As an albino. . ."he says 3 times
then says he's said it 3 times
but never finishes the. . .

"As an albino. . ."
& he's off again
trailing off into an. . .

I want do ask him
about Oberon & what
. . .went wrong?

still disguised
as a drunken human
he waves a hand unseeing

"These are our shadows. . ."
I whisper to myself
felling very Prospero...ish

our journey now
has parted
my next train is. . . late.

VENUSES IN TRANSIT

She's Venus in a shocking blue transit van
tapping fingers and toes to the radio song

"she's got it ohhhhh babyshe's got it. . .making every man a man.. ."

She enjoys being a plumber woman

seeing their faces when she turns up.

"Venus in blue jeans"
"Yeah. . ." she chortles ". . .that's me!"

"Mannnnnn.....damnnnnnnnn....these traffic light!"

She's Venus...nothing but a flash of ebony
hurtling after an orb of yellow

calculating the trajectory of the second
it left big sister Serena's wicked backhand.

"Mnnnnnnn....dammmmmmm....blAMMMMMM!"

Advantage Venus. New balls please.

She's Venus with her tiny eclipses of that big old sun.
I anxiously awaiting her return.

"I missed the first one and mannnnnnnn. . .
. . . damn if I am gonna miss the second one tooooooo!"

But at least I can't be worse than poor old Guillaume Le Gentil
spending 8 unsuccessful years trying to observe her
only to lose wife and possessions and be declared dead.

Wow...she's my Venus...my desire and. . ..awwwwwww
mannnnnnnnn damnnnnnnnn those clouds!

JESUS - THE EARLY YEARS

Jesus hits his thumb
"Language Jesus...language!"
Mary scolds him

Jesus just can't
get that dovetail joint...right
Joseph sighs

never bothering to learn
how to swim
Jesus just walks upon the water

Jesus turns the wine to water
"You've got it the wrong way 'round again!"
Jesus mutters under his breath

Jesus
turns the wine
into water

*

Inspired by a visit to Stanley Spenser's Cookham! Where the Bible is
incorporated into the ordinary everyday life of the village and the
miracle is the everyday blossoming forth in all its glory.

THIS MAN WHO IS NOT MY FATHER IS MY FATHER

This man who is not my father. . .is my father.

The others laugh:
"It's not your turn but he calls only for you! "

And so I go & clean him up his skeleton thin body
splashed with urine & shit.

I laugh & joke with him . . . he chuckles as I tell him:

"Michael...you used to be so full of crap but shit...now you're not! "

Lucky our Irish sense of humour extends this far
say anything with love and it becomes so.

It is a tired old joke but like a child he pounces on its nuances
relishing each pause and stupid syllable!

I bathe him this man who is not my father gently as if he were
. . . .my child.

I sing to him all the old songs
I learned at my father's hands as he bathed me.

"...why does my poor heart keep following you..."

We sing together softly as I bathe him dress him anew
in the memory of my father.

This man who is not my father becomes my father
as my hands learn to care for him.

I settle a pillow behind his head wipe sweat from his forehead
stroke his hair until his sleep is full of dreams...dreams.

TIME WORKS DIFFERENTLY FOR GRANDMOTHERS

I remember your father
kicking in my womb.

The sunshine fell on the floor
as if it were worshipping me.

I felt just like I was
the Virgin Mary or something

being told what was what

in some Renaissance painting by some guy whose
name I can't even pronounce.

"Woah there...little one! "
I said chuckling to the kicking.

"There's still time enough...less of the rough stuff! "
I tried to coax it into quietness.

"Don't be in such...a hurry...I'll still be here! "
I smiled to it and myself.

Then I had breakfast of coffee & scrambled egg & chives
with a little dill & paprika sprinkled on top.

Went on making baby for all I was worth.
The paprika would explain the red hair!

God...when it came...it was a difficult birth.
Felt like a peach...split apart.

Beethoven came into the room
from some passing car radio

& then floated out again
as if he were gliding around on his own notes.

I tried to follow where the music was going
but it got entangled in next door's clothes line.

A pigeon walked up & down the window sill
trying to look as if he was very busy but he was only

passing time &...poo!

"Shoo! " I scolded it and then wondered
what a pigeon would look like in a nappy.

Need a lot of changing!

I took a stray feather from a pillow
balanced it on my swollen belly

(God I was...huge!)

& laughed as it got kicked off.

"That's my girl! "
I grinned

'cos I was sure I was having a girl
but instead I was having your father.

Always never knew where I was with him.

He was always his own person
even when he hardly even existed.

Then when he handed me you
& I realised my baby's had a baby

I just cried & cried ...'till I laughed.

THE GEOGRAPHY OF BABY SITTING

she stands on
the open atlas
a foot on each continent

plops herself down
on middle America
wee wees run like rivers

"na na na naw!"
she gnaws
the east coast of Australia

geography studies
and baby sitting
at odds with each other

baby sitting
baby sits
on the world

the world
lies at her feet
she dances on oceans

like a little colossus
why man she doth bestride the world

I scoop her up for bedtime

CHOCOLATE EXPLANATIONS

"Right...! "

I try to explain it with chocolates

that she(girlishly) keeps trying to eat.

I pick a luscious dark chocolate seahorse and I say: "Now this is..."

(and she finishes my sentence for me)

"...your hippocampus! "

She squeals... delighted with herself.

"That's correct! " I praise her

"...it's shaped like this seahorse! "

"And it controls your memories of you

your "who you are"

your "how your self assembles its sense of self

...with all its past and future mysteries! "

"Yes...yes...that's it!

She claps her hands thrilled to bits

by the familiar telling .. .the reassurance of sounds.

And this twisted twirl of almond with a real almond in its center

"... is your amygdala! "

She blurts out before me.

"You got it" I smile.

"Everyone's got one!. . . a seahorse & an almond

 one on each side of our brain."

"Now the almond tells you how to respond to the things

that you've assembled into a sense of self

...with the proper emotion ...the right feeling.

...whether you just like or love it"

"Oh, I love it...I love it! "

She almost sings.

"Now, explain it to me again! "

I give her the finished explanations and she eats them

with much exaggerated mmmmming & ohhhhhing.

"I love your explanations

about what's wrong with my thingy"

She knocks upon her head like it was a door

to a self that she had locked herself outside of.

Most times she doesn't even know

her name

or who

or what

she is.

But she loves this story of

HIPPOCAMPUS AND ITS FAITHFUL AMYGDALA

She loves each sound each word each letter each pause

of the chocolate explanations.

CRAZY LONELINESS HIJACKS MEMORY
OF A BEAUTIFUL GIRL

Last night I missed you so much

I made love to your nightdress passionately.

Now your nightdress hides from me

slinks under covers and pillows. . .avoids my eyes.

I can't take another night without you!

Your nightie can't take another night with me!

I am holding your dresses hostage threatening them with
kisses...caresses if they make one false move.

Your other clothes

tremble in the wardrobe

...come back to me!

DONALL! DONALL!

'Dónall Dónall'

You not only pronounced me beautifully
rolled me 'round on your tongue

but curiously doubled it to - 'Dónall Dónall'

I used to love my name
tangled up in your laughter

I used to love my name
meshed up with your kisses

I used to love my name
repeated over and over

on the tip of your tongue
in the flash of your smile.

Memory (like a ventriloquist)
still plays tricks

that lovely lost last photo of you
fallen from a book fallen to the floor

I swear... it whispered: 'Dónall Dónall.'
...just once more.

WE ARE LEGEND...WE ARE MYTH

"DonallSeanie...SeanieDonall!"
My uncle & me

we are legend we are myth

escaping from my auntie's voice
tracking us down

I sitting in the saddle of his neck
his curls my reins

traveling the world
on his giant shoulders

my uncle hearing voices in his head
afraid of other humans who hunt the thoughts

he's thinking
wanting to keep himself for himself

our beings fused
into one joyfulness

uncle & boy morphing into centaur
we are legend we are myth

we hide in haystacks from her hounding voice

roam fields where ever empty spaces takes us until there is only us
he more little boy than even I

"Keep me company!"
he pleaded

his thoughts all curly like his hair

we now one another

the last lost centaur galloping off into a time
that no longer exists

we are legend. . .we are myth.

*

and the boy grew out of my head
where I had stuffed him on my shoulders

and I became his walker of worlds
galloping across fields

running away from the voices inside my head
that eat my thoughts

this boy I uncle
has become my mind for me. . .minds me

soothes the voices lies to the voices tells them I have vanished
into the mystery of myself and the voices fall for it

I watch them retreat I move my feet In giant steps

the boy growing out of my head sees the world for me
tames the world for me

so that I can laugh whinny & neigh like the human horse I have become no
longer confused fused into one being

him & me drinking in a sunset

sniffing rain on the wind galloping across time… time. . . time
time out of mind

CLOTHES HAVE NO MEMORIES

Your most prized dress must confess
that it cannot remember

the swell of your breast
the rise & fall of your breathing.

Clothes have no memory.

It is winter now and your summer
frock has totally forgot

the sheer sunny shockingness of being
(underneath it all) absolutely knickerless.

Kisses like butterflies alight high (high)
on your inner thigh (thigh)!

Clothes have no memory.

Your bra
unhooked & unhinged

cannot really recall
the thrill of it all

as my hands caress
create your breasts.

Clothes have no memory.

Clothes have no memory
...but I do.

www.ingramcontent.com/pod-product-compliance
Lightning Source LLC
LaVergne TN
LVHW091209080426
835509LV00006B/906